Drink of Sensation

Brenaye Powell

BookLeaf
Publishing

India | USA | UK

Presentation by *BookLeaf Publishing*

Web: www.bookleafpub.com

E-mail: info@bookleafpub.com

ISBN: 9789357617895

First edition 2023

This is dedicated to McKinley "Sonny" Rogers and Marvin "Bobo" Lindsey. Thank you for loving me. I hope I make you proud.

PREFACE

Creating a book of poetry was a restorative experience. I have always found release in putting my thoughts down on paper. The poems written come from personal experiences of being a single mother, the loss of both of my sons' fathers, mother-daughter relationships, and finding my biological father at the age of 40. These poems were constructed late at night or in the wee hours of the morning, outside of work, home and college courses to complete my associate's degree. I am excited to share my thoughts and hope you find my perspectives eye-opening and relatable.

Full Circle

Who will this strange, small creature grow up to
be?
Allah/Abba paved her path, before she could
even see.
Regal are the ways that she learned to think,
live, and breathe,
Rightly so! It was all the time she spent praying
for substance on her knees, aggrieved.
Ignited by purpose to right what was wrong
Opulent with mercy and grace, she was destined
to stand strong!

Riveting rivers of life undulate from her aura
Erupting power forged through the experience
plethora
Saccharine is her name, no longer sullied; she
has fought life and been victorious!! for
She is me..a glorious divine WARRIORESS!

Listen

Open your ears and your hearts. The things
being said will help guide you when you start
out on your own, I won't leave you alone, blind,
and deaf to roam, looking to belong.

Love, hurt, joy, pain memories reverberating
through synapses in the brain. Flashes of
lessons learned, and bridges burned
tears in steaming showers, falling like rain.

I did so you wouldn't have to. I bent so I
wouldn't break you, I ran so all you had to do
was stand, tall and true. The plan is to pass the
baton on to you, with such an easy lead, I
thought the worse was through.

Head high, chest out, shoulders back…keep
moving
Heart stings, broken things.. keep improving
Trial and error, fair-weather, growing is
bittersweet but that's the purpose little ones, to
ensure to plant your feet on concrete… LISTEN

Morning

Quiet mornings before dawn, the stillness, the
calm, adorning my soul like a sweet fragrant
balm.
Deep breaths of crisp clean air, the wind blowing
through my hair, filling my lungs, stretching like
flowers reaching for the sun.
Quiet mornings before dawn, the stillness, the
calm, adorning my soul like a sweet fragrant
balm.
Silent prayers of forgiveness, thankfulness,
wisdom and peace, my steps being ordered by
the song that's released.
The day will be dawning soon, new
opportunities and lessons await. Birds are
chirping, music they make, our songs collide,
they interrelate.

Quiet mornings before dawn, the stillness, the calm, adorning my soul like a sweet fragrant balm.

Expectancy in the morning, after a night of ravaged tears, swollen eyes, stuffy nose, trying to hide from my fears.

Reassured that there is still so much work to do, renewed, blessed with breath and beating heart, it's a sign to continue to PUSH through.

Quiet mornings before dawn, the stillness, the calm, adorning my soul like a sweet fragrant balm.

Span of Time

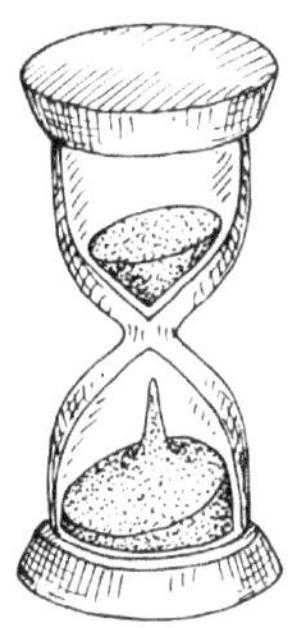

A couch sitting in the intersection of an empty street, surrounded by tall buildings on all sides, just before dawn breaks.

Sun rays finally reach a corner of the couch, after fighting to crest the buildings, and slowly expose more details; tattered and worn, a rip here, a stain there. A woman sitting at the far end, still in the shadows, awaiting the sun's rays.

Who is this woman?

As the sun's rays start to warm her skin, other
figures move in and out of the lines of vision, all
surrounding the couch, talking, singing, playing,
praying, loving, being.

Fingertips caress her cheek, a hand rubs the
small of her back; their fingers intertwine,
butterfly kisses on soft lips, whispers of love and
forever...rocking a sleepy baby, wiping a runny
nose, cuddling with a warm blanket - little
hands, little toes; popcorn and a favorite movie,
pizza night with friends, feet propped up with a
glass of wine to bring the weekend in,
conversations with friends, life decisions to
make, plans notated, journal entries made...

The sunlight starts to fade, creeping again
behind buildings. Shadows crawl across the
couch, whispers, promises, prayers, affirmations,
declarations; tomorrow the sun will shine again.

What is a Mess

I detest the mess of a teenager's room.
Clothes strewn here and there, is that a pair of
underwear?
Cups and bowls, with discarded food, who are
they feeding? I wonder as I brood.
Notebook paper, scraps with half completed and
graded assignments, the trashcan in the corner is
in perfect alignment.

Let's not forget the dirty socks and rumpled
clothes, the smell alone could take down any
foe, oh the woe!
And they know I'm going to throw a fit, because
I did not raise them like this! They don't
comprehend the lessons I've given; they won't
understand until they have their own children...
Pick up your mess, place things back where you
got them, it makes life easier than me hooting
and hollering...
Sweep and mop the wooden floors, put all
washed and folded clothes in your drawers, keep
your rooms clean, just do your chores...please.

Keep Going

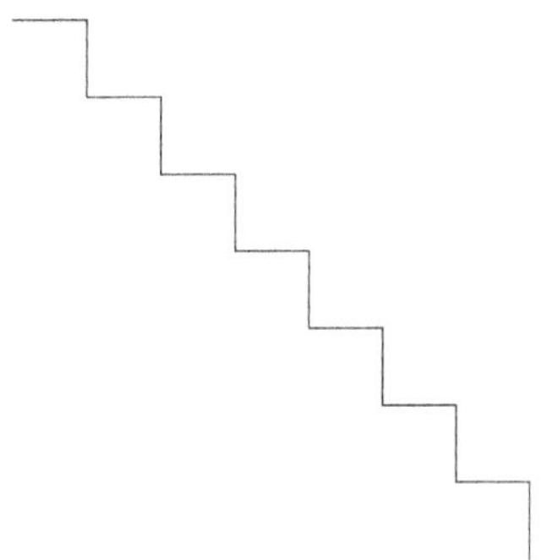

Living is what we do! Every day is brand new,
there is so much in store, so much to explore, so
many wonders; what lies behind the next door?
I pray for peace, a prayer for generational curses
to be broken, for prosperity and hope; every
demon I'm choking!
My life has not been in vain, divine is my name,
I will finish what I started, everything God
imparted.

Not my will, but his be done, I have already overcome so much through him, my light will not dim.

I am aware, I am open, to conquer all like he spoke, and be the light, get it right all the lessons that he was throwing. I caught them, I didn't falter, look at my daughter and my sons....still the battle is not won. We March ON!

This Is Not Goodbye

I miss you.
I miss your smile and your laugh, I miss your
spirit, fighting hard to last.
There were arguments and fights as couples do,
but I would trade it all just to have you.
I look at them and I see you, I try so hard, but no
one can replace what they knew.
Secure, understood, growing young boys and a
young girl; How can I prepare them for this
world by myself? I need help!

Not a day goes by, that you haven't crossed my
mind, sometimes blind with the tears they can't
see fall down.
Stay strong they say, move on they say, but how
can you when what you loved was taken away?
What do the little ones actually see, in me, when
my place was secure in thee?

I keep moving, I push forward, I guide them, I
taught them.
Do they know how much I hurt, not having you
on this earth?
Am I doing this right, am I teaching them light, I
don't want them to go wrong, I would rather it be
right.
Cancer sucks! Congestive heart failure sucks...I
hate them both, NOT GIVING NO FUCKS!! I
pray things turn out according to his will for us.
In God we trust, it's a must.

Love

I love to love it is a beautiful thing, not
something that was taught to me easily. It was
hard fought through blood, sweat, and tears, it
took years for me to conquer my fears, and heal.
I've lived my life in survival mode, it's difficult
to remain composed through the day-to-day
obstacles. But I have to be bold!
The garments of shame, denial, of people
pleasing them more than me have retired.

I craved her love, her affection, like a drug, it
always eluded me like everything else swept
under the rug.
But no more! My life is to be lived and there is
so much more in store.
I forgive, no regret, no grudges, no more
transgressions directed in the wrong direction. I
looked within and found I held all the blessings
needed to be me. Needed to grow, needed to see,
needed to live, needed to breathe.
Love is a beautiful thing, I finally learned to
love me. Love is my testimony.

You

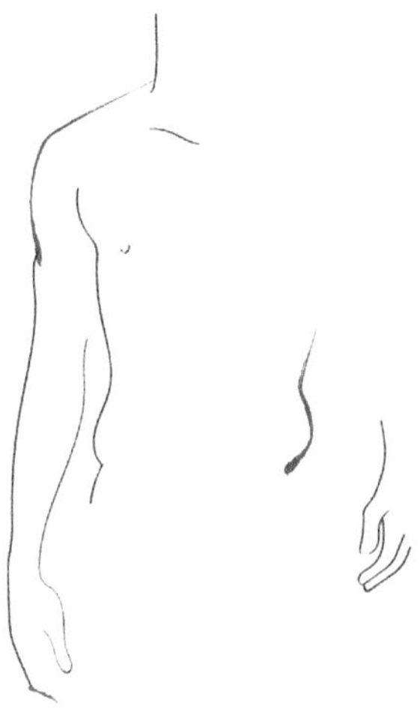

I had the best dream.
You came to see me.
It was just like old times, we laughed, we joked,
I cried...
We went to a concert, we were on t.v., you never
left my side, you were right there with me.
The concert was over, the crowd was let out, I
was tousled and bumped, pushed away from you
by the throng, I could see your head over the
crowd, mouthing "It's ok, stay strong".

I emerged from the arena, and turned looking for
your face, I found you and we embraced.
Then fast forward, still in this embrace, we were
in our room, your hands and lips kissing my
face. I asked about the kids and you said they
were just fine; I stood before you exposed,
naked, you stepped back to get a full look at me
and said "Divine".
You turned me around to face the mirror, your
chest to my back, and your arms around me,
there we stood just like that. And we rocked and
we swayed to the music in our head, and I was
warm and safe in your embrace, no reason to
dread.
And that's how I woke up, still wrapped in your
love, tears on pillowcases, smiles on faces when
you come to see me in my dreams, the sweetest
gift is being awakened by moonbeams. I miss
you my love, by all means you make yourself
seen.

To-Do List

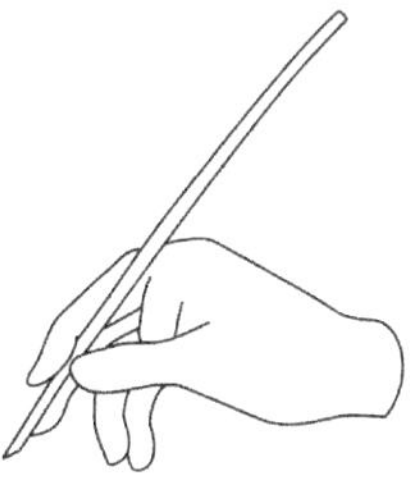

What a day today was, so much pressure, so
much stress...
My mind and my body need a rest after such a
strenuous test.

Between work and children, cooking and
cleaning, all normal things sure, but all together
I'm careening.

Little fires everywhere, back-to-back zoom
meetings, corporate dynamics, so exhausting the
bullshit, and I deserve better dammit!
Quietly quitting, that's a new thing, there's also
quiet firing - which one is occurring?

Pick up the children, field school calls and
questions, homework lessons, facial expressions
when asked to pick up their possessions. Dinner
is started, a load of clothes transported...the list
goes on, but I don't want to be sordid.

Just halfway done, there's still more to do, I have
homework, it's finals and my paper's not
through. I took a little time for me too; so, I
could also write this poem to you.

Children are fed, bathed and in bed, now it's
time for me...

Chemistry

Hey love, how are you doing? I'm glad you stopped by, it's been a long time since I've seen you, and you've been on my mind.

You pull me into your warm embrace, I place my head on your chest, listen to your heartbeat, breathe in your scent, your hands graze my back, I anticipate what awaits.

We're in the room, warm lips touching, kissing my neck, below my earlobe,

nip, lick, blow...shoulder kisses as you pull
down bra straps, limiting my movements the
tops of my breasts become your snack.

You turn me around, my back against your chest,
hands roaming, hearts beating, heavy
breathing...you unhook the confines of your
snack, and your fingers rub what your mouth
attracts, little blooms blossom where the bra was
at.

Shirt pulled over my head, bra discarded to the
floor, my fingers look for you, I want to feel you
too, I want more, my hands rub across your
chest, the little patch of hair under your neck, the
ridges and valleys are so smooth so divine, your
buds have blossomed too, nip, lick, blow... just
like mine.

We fall across the bed, exploring each other,
hands roaming, hearts beating, heavy
breathing...quiet eruptions of pleasure spill from
our mouths, anticipation growing, my body
primed, prepared to receive, my mind spinning
from your masculine energy.

Ecstasy... (rated PG-13)

And we're sated, unabated, wrapped together amongst sheets. nip, lick, blow, hands roaming, hearts beating, heavy breathing... until the next time we meet...

I Am Me

A Black woman in America.

You can't even imagine who she is, lots of
people think they know but wouldn't know
where to begin.

Being a single mom, they act like it was my
choice, I wanted the wedding, house and kids;
but it ended in divorce.

I didn't have time for remorse, my daughter
watched me with her bright innocent eyes, I
trusted love would find me again and God
blessed me with 2 boys, to my surprise.

And the boys' dads, he took to be with him, so
here I stand alone raising them.
No stable support system, no family in sight, but
God blessed me with friends to help me continue
to fight.

So not only do I contend with being a single
mom, being Black in America, it's a ticking time
bomb.

When I say what's on my mind, they feel I lack
empathy and understanding; it's just that I'm not
blind to the looks, behaviors, despair,
commanding... I should do this, I should do that,
look like this, act like that.... THIS SHIT IS
WACK!

Conversations with children on the differences
implanted, teaching and reaching for more

without balance. Does knowing they hate me,
make me a racist? Or is being aware my
day-to-day anelaces?

Everything takes more effort, more energy,
nothing comes easily except them being afraid
of or thinking they are better than me...

You can find me praying hard, dealing with the
onslaught of things that come my way and
thanking God to live each and every day, come
what may.

Daddy

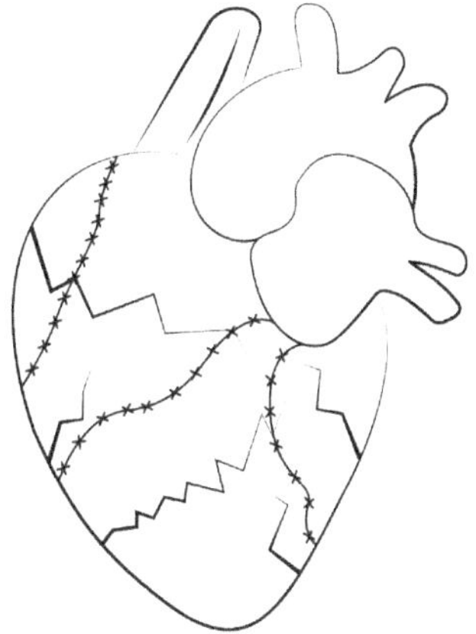

I wasted so much time trying to fit the image
others wanted.
It started long before I understood the dynamics
of being taunted.

I worked hard for her approval, all I wanted was
understanding
It was too much to ask of someone who was set
on reprimanding.

All I could comprehend is that something was
not right,
I'd fought, I cried, I tried to make her realize, but
my words were turned against me, they came out
contrite.

As I grew, I didn't notice that I carried this
emptiness with me. It was when I had my own
children, I wanted to get rid of the impertinence
from me.

Part of that process included finding the man she
said didn't want me...I didn't know where to
start, where to begin to heal so I might feel
complete.

More fights, more tears, more trying to make her
see, I needed information, I needed answers to
the things I was made to believe.

And God worked on me, mending my heart,
filling my soul, his mercy and his grace beautiful
to behold.

Time passed before I knew it, evolving into who
he created me to be, releasing fear, doubts,
shame, guilt: loving me unconditionally, I know
this life was made just for me...regardless of
claims made to deceive.

This personal growth fueled my path, projection
in place, I started the steps needed to close out
my paternity case.

Long story short, I found him with such ease, he
wasn't hiding at all, he didn't even know about
me.

Paternity confirmed 99.9998%, no denying the
truth, it always wins in the end.
I missed him since my youth, a new chapter we
can begin.

Meeting him it all made sense, everything
clicked; all my differences weren't different at
all because I fit in with them. It was like coming
home after a very long stint, that feeling of
belonging, something I'd always missed.

Down the Drain

I love the way it moves and flows over my body.
The way it slides and glides over my curves.
It fills us up oddly
All while preserving life here on earth.
The warmth it gives to ease tight muscles, or the
cooling it provides from sun rays shuffle.
I love sitting in its aromatic presence, relaxing in
lavender or mint.
Bubbles filled with healing pleasures; the steam
allows my soul to vent.

Release the stress and tension from the day, clear
my mind, let it all wash away.
Rejuvenated, refreshed to begin anew, all the
things water can do. Try it..it's true.

OCD

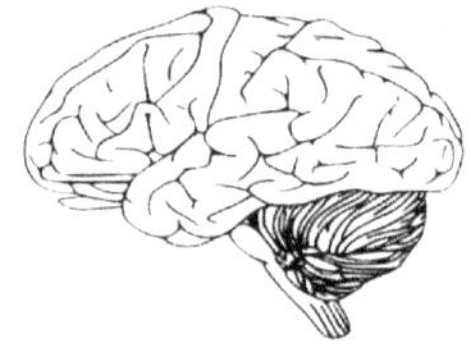

The fresh smell of clean is something
intoxicating to me.
Shiny mirrors and glass with no smudges or
fingerprints.
Polished wood and brass reflecting light like
anglerfish.

Dusting fans and light fixtures, changing air
vents to breathe clearer

Sweeping and mopping, can't forget vacuuming-
the lines in the carpet straight like soldiers in a
unit.

Dishes washed, dried and put away; plates
stacked neatly for dinner the next day. Clothes
washed, dried and folded, placed on hangers and
put away in the closet.

Fresh linen on beds, pillows fluffed, drapes
spread, bathtub scrubbed, toilet flushed, trash
tossed, what's next? Are the chores complete? Is
everything tidy, neat and put in its place? The
smell of clean is more than a scent, it's a
headspace.

Numb

There is this thing that I do, strictly for me, has nothing to do with you.
While growing and learning to work through different challenges; I developed these mechanisms...more like deterrents.

In order to numb myself from pain I grew a habit following the cigarette and alcohol campaign. The taste of a drink touching my lips, ignited nerves in my body that helped my mood shift. It didn't matter either wine, liquor, beer, it

was the fog that came with it, that made
everything seem clear. What was really
happening was me speaking uncouth, my tongue
inhibited, my soul disapproved.

To counter, I would tap a fresh pack of
cigarettes, to make sure the hit was strong when
I took a drag. To hold one between my fingers
and flick the lighter to its end, to see the flame
and embers, inhaling the toxins in. The rush of
nicotine created a balance to the alcohol in my
system; there it is, the numbness, what I was
chasing was not feeling.

No longer were these social queues used in
awkward spaces. They were now my crutches on
a day-to-day basis. Habits I grew to learn held
no power in the end, besides that of destroying
my body from within. This journey is not easy,
no one said it would be fair; but I'd rather do it
sober without cigarette smoke in my hair.
Beware!

We Live

Life is so fleeting, and it is so precious.
There is a lesson hidden within every secession.
How did we get here? What did we learn? What things were done that should never be done again?

We live, we love, we lose, we gain, we grow, we change.
Ebb and flow, up and down, in and out, roundabout we live.

So grateful, so thankful for mercy and grace to continue on every day. We live.

"M" Words

Morning - A fresh start, a clean slate, beginning again, breathing in the day.

Mercy - knowing without knowing, keeping me safe, covering, guiding, lighting my way.

Meaning - There are definitions, but do you agree? Right or wrong, true or false, what do you believe?

Meal - Large and grand, feast or fast, nourishment is what the body asks.

Music - A praise, a psalm, a rap or ballad, all from the soul, all are magic.